Paw Prints

Poodles

by Kaitlyn Duling

Bullfrog Books

Ideas for Parents and Teachers

Bullfrog Books let children practice reading informational text at the earliest reading levels. Repetition, familiar words, and photo labels support early readers.

Before Reading
- Discuss the cover photo. What does it tell them?
- Look at the picture glossary together. Read and discuss the words.

Read the Book
- "Walk" through the book and look at the photos. Let the child ask questions. Point out the photo labels.
- Read the book to the child, or have him or her read independently.

After Reading
- Prompt the child to think more. Ask: Have you ever seen a poodle? Would you like to play with one?

Bullfrog Books are published by Jump!
5357 Penn Avenue South
Minneapolis, MN 55419
www.jumplibrary.com

Copyright © 2019 Jump! International copyright reserved in all countries. No part of this book may be reproduced in any form without written permission from the publisher.

Library of Congress Cataloging-in-Publication Data

Names: Duling, Kaitlyn, author.
Title: Poodles / by Kaitlyn Duling.
Description: Minneapolis, MN : Jump!, Inc., 2018.
Series: Paw prints
Series: Bullfrog books | Includes index.
Audience: Ages 5 to 8. | Audience: Grades K to 3.
Identifiers: LCCN 2017041230 (print)
LCCN 2017043184 (ebook)
ISBN 9781624967818 (ebook)
ISBN 9781624967801 (hardcover : alk. paper)
Subjects: LCSH: Poodles—Juvenile literature.
Classification: LCC SF429.P85 (ebook)
LCC SF429.P85 D85 2018 (print) | DDC 636.72/8—dc23
LC record available at https://lccn.loc.gov/2017041230

Editor: Jenna Trnka
Book Designer: Molly Ballanger

Photo Credits: Agency Animal Picture/Getty, cover; Susan Schmitz/Shutterstock, 1; Jagodka/Shutterstock, 3, 8 (left), 9 (right); Teemu Tretiakov/Shutterstock, 4; digibabe/iStock, 5; Jean Michel Labat/Pantheon/SuperStock, 6–7 (foreground), 23tr; ayarosfaii/Shutterstock, 6–7 (background); Eric Isselee/Shutterstock, 8 (right), 22; Nikolai Tsvetkov/Shutterstock, 9 (left), 23tl; paylessimages/iStock, 10–11; Natalia V Guseva/Shutterstock, 12–13; Tribune Content Agency LLC/Alamy, 14–15, 23br; Debby Wong/Shutterstock, 16–17, 23bl; StockphotoVideo/Shutterstock, 18; Jne Valokuvaus/Shutterstock, 19; Stockbyte/Getty, 20–21 (foreground); Michal Chmurski/Shutterstock, 20–21 (background); Toloubaev Stanislav/Shutterstock, 24.

Printed in the United States of America at Corporate Graphics in North Mankato, Minnesota.

Table of Contents

Three Sizes	4
A Poodle Up Close	22
Picture Glossary	23
Index	24
To Learn More	24

Three Sizes

What is that dog?

It is curly.

It is a poodle!

There are three sizes.
What are they?
Toy. Miniature. Standard.

They are different colors, too.

White. Black. Gray. Tan.

Their hair is thick.

It is curly.

Some have funny haircuts. Why?

They were bred to retrieve.

They swim.

Short hair helps them swim better.

But some hair keeps them warm.

Some are in dog shows.
Their owners walk them.
They show them off.

These dogs are very smart. This one dances!

This one jumps over a bar! Wow!

Poodles are fun.

Do you want to play with one?

A Poodle Up Close

Picture Glossary

bred
Developed as a dog breed.

miniature
A smaller version of something.

dog shows
Competitions at which dogs are judged on their performance and appearance.

retrieve
To get something and bring it back.

Index

colors 8	jumps 19
curly 5, 10	retrieve 14
dances 18	sizes 7
dog shows 17	smart 18
hair 10, 13, 14	swim 14
haircuts 13	thick 10

To Learn More

Learning more is as easy as 1, 2, 3.

1) Go to www.factsurfer.com

2) Enter "poodles" into the search box.

3) Click the "Surf" button to see a list of websites.

With factsurfer.com, finding more information is just a click away.